The Ganges

India's Sacred River

By Molly Aloian

CRABTREE
Publishing Company
www.crabtreebooks.com

Crabtree Publishing Company
www.crabtreebooks.com

Author: Molly Aloian
Editor: Barbara Bakowski
Designer: Tammy West, Westgraphix LLC
Photo Researcher: Edward A. Thomas
Map Illustrator: Stefan Chabluk
Indexer: Nila Glikin
Project Coordinator: Kathy Middleton
Crabtree Editor: Adrianna Morganelli
Production Coordinator: Kenneth Wright
Prepress Technician: Kenneth Wright

Series Consultant: Michael E. Ritter, Ph.D., Professor
of Geography, University of Wisconsin—Stevens Point

Developed for Crabtree Publishing Company by RJF
Publishing LLC (www.RJFpublishing.com)

Photo Credits:
Cover: White/Photolibrary
4: © Keith Taylor/Alamy
6, 15, 17, 24, 26: iStockphoto
7: Peter Adams/The Image Bank/Getty Images
8: © EyeUbiquitous/Alamy
11 (top): Jeff Speigner/Shutterstock
11 (bottom): JH Pete Carmichael/The Image Bank/
    Getty Images;
12: Carlos Arguelles/ Shutterstock
14: © Nordicphotos/Alamy
15: Chris Caldicott/Axion Photographic Agency/
    Getty Images;
18: Nicholas DeVore/Stone/Getty Images
19, 25: AFP/Getty Images
21: SSPL via Getty Images
23: © Alexei Fateev/ Alamy

Cover: The Ganges River flows through the Indian city of
Varanasi, where thousands of Hindus bathe each day in the
river they consider sacred.

Library and Archives Canada Cataloguing in Publication

Aloian, Molly
    The Ganges : India's sacred river / Molly Aloian.

(Rivers around the world)
Includes index.
ISBN 978-0-7787-7443-3 (bound).--ISBN 978-0-7787-7466-2 (pbk.)

    1. Ganges River (India and Bangladesh)--Juvenile literature.
2. Ganges River Valley (India and Bangladesh)--Juvenile literature.
I. Title. II. Series: Rivers around the world

DS485.G25A46 2010   j954.'1   C2009-906239-9

Library of Congress Cataloging-in-Publication Data

Aloian, Molly.

The Ganges : India's sacred river / by Molly Aloian.
    p. cm. -- (Rivers around the world)
Includes index.
 ISBN 978-0-7787-7466-2 (pbk. : alk. paper) -- ISBN 978-0-7787-7443-3
(reinforced library binding : alk. paper)
1. Ganges River (India and Bangladesh)--Juvenile literature. 2.
Ganges River Valley (India and Bangladesh)--Juvenile literature. I.
Title. II. Series.

DS485.G25A66 2009
954'.1--dc22
                                                    2009042405

Crabtree Publishing Company
www.crabtreebooks.com   1-800-387-7650

Printed in the U.S.A./122009/BG20091103

Published in Canada
Crabtree Publishing
616 Welland Ave.
St. Catharines, ON
L2M 5V6

Published in the United States
Crabtree Publishing
PMB 59051
350 Fifth Avenue, 59th Floor
New York, New York 10118

**Published in the United
Kingdom**
Crabtree Publishing
Maritime House
Basin Road North, Hove
BN41 1WR

Published in Australia
Crabtree Publishing
386 Mt. Alexander Rd.
Ascot Vale (Melbourne)
VIC 3032

CONTENTS

Words that are defined in the glossary are in **bold** type
the first time they appear in the text.

CHAPTER 1
Sacred River

The Ganges River is the lifeblood of hundreds of millions of people in India and Bangladesh. Every day, they depend on its water for drinking, cooking, and washing. Farmers rely on the river for water for their crops. **Hindus** worship the Ganges River as a goddess named Ganga. Yet this river is threatened by pollution and by the increasing water demands of industries, cities, and a growing population.

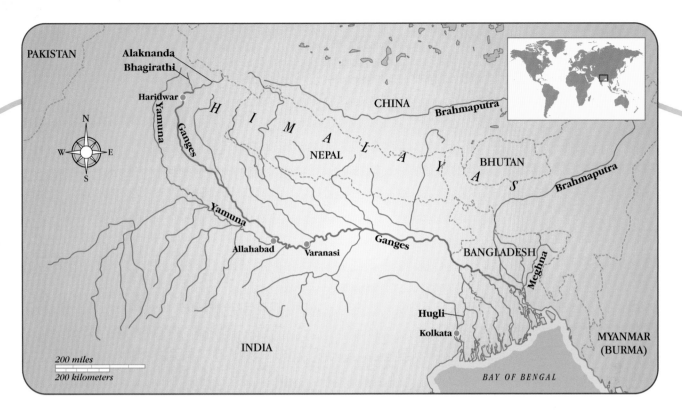

The Ganges River flows 1,560 miles (2,510 km) from its source in the Himalayas to its mouth at the Bay of Bengal.

A Shared River

The Ganges River begins in the Himalayas, the highest mountain range in the world. The river flows southeast across the plains of northern India. It then enters Bangladesh and is joined by the Brahmaputra River and the Meghna River. There the river's name changes to the Padma River. It forms a **delta** 220 miles (350 kilometers) wide, which is shared by India and Bangladesh. Finally, the river empties into the Bay of Bengal.

In comparison with many other major world rivers, the Ganges River is short, with a length of about 1,560 miles (2,510 km). For most of its course, the river is wide and its waters are slow-moving.

FAST FACT
The Ganges River **drainage basin** covers about 400,000 square miles (one million square km).

LEFT: The Ganges River is central to the lives of millions of people in India and Bangladesh.

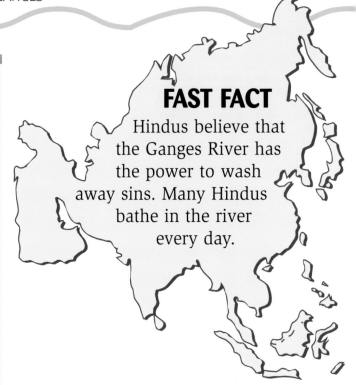

The Ganges River is fed by glaciers high in the Himalayan mountain range.

Glacial Waters

The main sources of the Ganges River are the Bhagirathi River and the Alaknanda River. The water in these rivers comes from **glaciers** high in the Himalayas. Melting glacial ice sustains the Ganges River and its **tributaries**.

Heavy Rains

Monsoon rains play a major role in the life of the Ganges River and in the lives of the people who live along its banks. Crop production depends on the monsoons. The monsoons begin in June, and the wettest month is August. During August, monsoons can bring up to 20 inches (51 centimeters) of rain. The monsoons can cause terrible floods in the Ganges delta region.

A Variety of Life

From its mountain source to its wide delta, the Ganges River flows through a variety of **ecosystems**. Many different types of animals live in and along the river. Some of these animals live nowhere else on Earth; they have adapted to life in this environment. The Ganges River and its tributaries are home to the endangered Ganges river dolphin. The rare Bengal tiger lives in the delta region, where it hunts buffalo, deer, wild pigs, and other large mammals.

NOTABLE QUOTE
"The Gang[es]…has been a symbol of India's age-long culture and civilization, ever changing, ever flowing, and yet ever the same."

—Jawaharlal Nehru, first prime minister of India

Many Hindus bathe daily in the Ganges River at the ancient city of Varanasi, in India.

Plant life is also varied. High in the Himalayas, the Ganges River flows through a forested region. The flat plains through which the river flows have been mostly cleared for farming, so little of the region's natural plant cover remains. Much of the delta region is covered by a thick forest of mangrove trees.

The Center of Life

Human civilizations have relied on the Ganges River for thousands of years. Historically, the river has been the center of the cultural, social, religious, and **economic** lives of vast numbers of people. The river flows through a region known as Hindustan, the site of successive civilizations from the third century BC through the 1500s AD.

Today, hundreds of millions of people depend on the Ganges River for their survival. Its basin is one of the most densely populated areas of the world. The river provides fish to eat, supplies water to drink, and makes transportation possible. It is used to generate electricity, supply water for crop **irrigation**, and carry away both human and industrial waste. **Cremation** of the dead along the sacred Ganges River is common practice for Hindus.

CHAPTER 2
The River Basin

Many scientists divide the Ganges River basin into three different zones: the Himalayan zone, the Gangetic plain zone, and the delta zone. Life in and around the river is different in each zone.

Himalayan Zone

The Himalayan zone includes the **headstreams** of the Ganges River, in the southern part of the mountain range. The Bhagirathi River begins in a cave at 10,000 feet (3,000 meters) above sea level. The water leaves the cave and drops into the Bhaironghati **gorge**. Forests of cedar, birch, oak, and pine border the river, whose clear waters flow fast.

The other main source, the Alaknanda River, begins at an altitude of 25,600 feet (7,800 m). It joins the Bhagirathi River at Devprayag, which is a town in the state of Uttarakhand, India. From that point, the river is known as the Ganges River.

Gangetic Plain Zone

In the flat Gangetic plain zone, the river flows south and then turns east, flowing more slowly. When the Ganges River is joined by several major tributaries, its volume of water increases. The soil in this region is very fertile. During monsoon season, the river overflows and deposits **silt** along its banks. Farmers grow rice and wheat in the Gangetic plain, one of the most productive agricultural regions in the world.

Delta Zone

In the delta zone, the river begins to fan out. It forms a delta 220 miles (350 km) wide at the Bay of Bengal. The delta was created from billions of tons of silt picked up and carried along by the Ganges River. Part of the delta lies in Bangladesh, and part in India.

Shaping the Land

About 50 million years ago, drifting Indian and **Eurasian** landmasses smashed together, causing huge areas of land to be pushed upward. The jagged peaks of the Himalayas were formed. At that time, the Gangetic plain was a deep valley at the base of the mountains. Over time, rivers that ran down the mountains deposited **sediment** in the valley, building it up into a wide, level plain.

Down the Drain

The Ganges River drains, or carries away the surface water from, about

LEFT: The Alaknanda and Bhagirathi rivers meet at Devprayag, in India, forming the Ganges River.

one-fourth of the land in India.

A **drainage pattern** is the arrangement of a main stream and its tributaries. The Ganges River has a **dendritic** drainage pattern, which looks like the branches of a tree.

Plant Life

More than 40,000 species of plants grow in India, and at least half of them can be found along the Ganges River and in its basin. Forests of pine, spruce, and other trees thrive in the Himalayan zone. India's national plant, the banyan tree, grows in the Gangetic plain zone. The banyan can reach a height of 100 feet (30 m). Aerial roots

How Much Rain?

In August, during the monsoon in India, the Himalayan zone receives 16 to 20 inches (40 to 50 cm) of rain. The delta zone receives 16 to 18 inches (40 to 46 cm). During monsoon season, the banks of the Ganges River are flooded.

grow down from its leafy branches, taking root in the soil and forming new trunks. The large mangrove woodland in the delta zone is called the Sundarbans. It is the largest mangrove forest in the world. Mangrove trees have jumbled, arching roots.

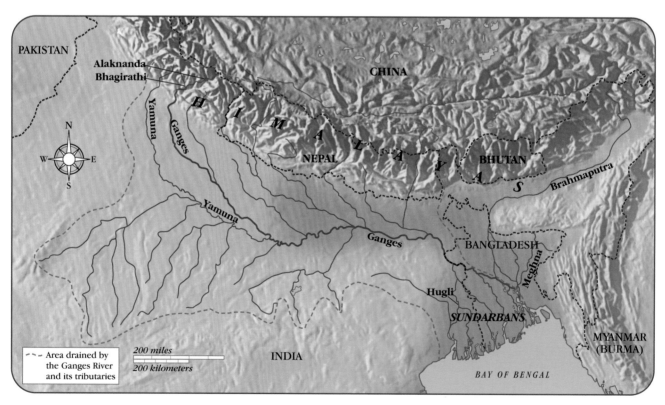

The Ganges River and its tributaries drain about 400,000 square miles (one million square km) of land.

India's national plant, the banyan tree, can live for hundreds of years.

Amazing Animals

Many animals live in the Ganges River, including more than 100 species of fish. The gray Ganges river dolphin is from seven to eight feet (two to 2.5 m) long. The dolphin probes the muddy river bottom with its flipper and its long snout in search of shrimp and fish to eat. The Ganges shark is a rarely sighted and highly endangered species of freshwater shark.

In the Himalayan zone, brown bears, red pandas, and snow leopards occasionally visit the river to drink and hunt for food. Deer, crocodiles, and monkeys inhabit the delta zone. The Bengal tiger also calls this area home, but it is threatened by **poachers**.

Gangetic Gharial

The gharial is a species of crocodile that lives in the Gangetic plain zone. This reptile uses its long, slender snout and sharp teeth to catch fish in fast-moving waters. The gharial can grow to be 20 feet (six m) long. It is an endangered species.

The Gangetic gharial nests on sandbanks along the Ganges River.

CHAPTER 3

People of the Ganges

Thousands of years ago, Indian civilizations developed in the Ganges basin because the river provided for people's needs. The Ganges River provided water for drinking and for growing food crops. The river was also an important transportation route. Flooding deposited nutrients that left the soil rich for farming. Cities grew up in the fertile Ganges plain as an economy based on agriculture developed.

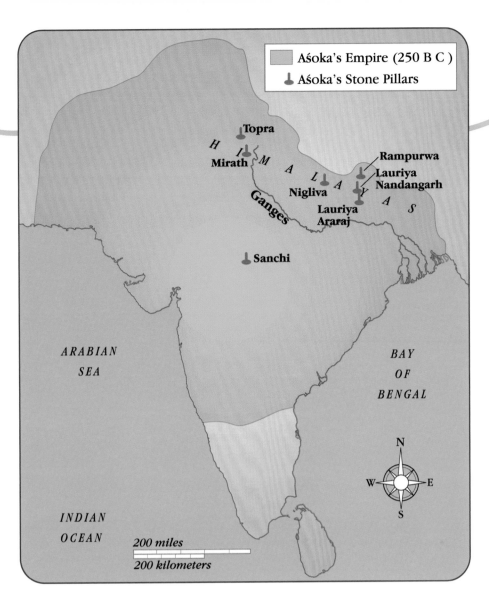

The Mauryan Empire reached its greatest extent during the rule of Aśoka.

The Mauryan Empire

Agriculture was an important part of the economy of the Mauryan Empire (about 322 BC to 185 BC). The state owned huge farms, which were worked by slaves and farm laborers. Farmers planted a variety of hardy crops, including types of grains, peas, and beans. These crops required only minimal water and **cultivation**.

LEFT: The Ganges River has long been an important travel and transportation route.

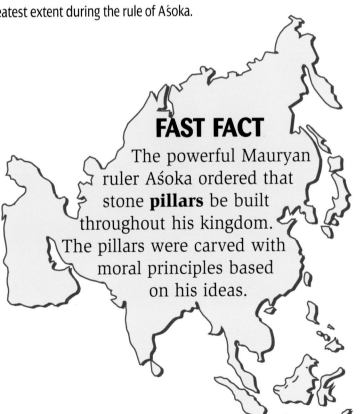

FAST FACT

The powerful Mauryan ruler Aśoka ordered that stone **pillars** be built throughout his kingdom. The pillars were carved with moral principles based on his ideas.

13

Holy Sites

Hindu priests designated special holy places, called tirthas, along the banks of the Ganges River at the cities of Haridwar, Allahabad, and Varanasi. At Haridwar, the river meets the Gangetic plain. Allahabad is at the **confluence** of the Ganges and Yamuna rivers. The third tirtha is in the ancient city of Varanasi. Every day, tens of thousands of Hindus bathe on the ghats, or stone steps, that lead down to the Ganges River at Varanasi.

Hindus celebrate a religious festival in Haridwar, India.

A bold war leader named Chandragupta Maurya founded the Mauryan Empire. Chandragupta's grandson, Aśoka, expanded the area under his control, making it the largest empire in ancient Indian history. Aśoka is known for his belief in the **Buddhist** ideals of nonviolence and charity. Buddhism is a religion that developed in northern India between the sixth and fourth centuries BC.

The top of an Aśokan pillar.

The Mauryan Empire began to decline in 232 BC after Aśoka's death. Within 50 years, it had ceased to exist.

The Gupta Empire

The Gupta Empire flourished from 320 AD to 550 AD. Its rulers controlled much of the land that had made up the earlier Mauryan Empire. This period is sometimes called the

A Hindu temple stands on the banks of the Ganges River in Uttarakhand, India.

Golden Age of India because many advances were made in science. Painters, poets, and musicians also thrived. Artisans made clay river goddesses to show their respect for the Ganges River and other rivers. Trade also increased during this period.

Fishing and Hunting

Ancient people relied on the Ganges River not only for farming but also for fish. **Archaeologists** have found evidence of ancient metal fish hooks. They have also discovered ancient paintings that show fishing boats with nets extended on both sides. As the boats moved through the water, people dipped the nets into the river. Fish were trapped and then hauled aboard. Ancient people also hunted birds and crocodiles that lived along the banks of the Ganges River.

Religion and the River

For more than 3,500 years, Hindus have worshipped the Ganges River. Present-day Hinduism is a major world religion that traces its roots to ancient India.

Early Hindus believed that drinking or bathing in the waters of the Ganges River would bring spiritual rewards. An ancient Hindu poem reveals that birth itself was believed to be a gift of

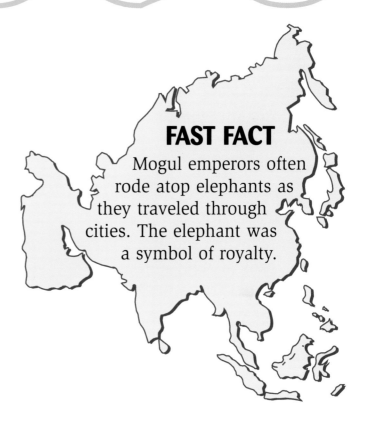

FAST FACT
Mogul emperors often rode atop elephants as they traveled through cities. The elephant was a symbol of royalty.

the river. The poem states: "He who was born of old was born of water. Right from the waters, the soul drew forth and shaped a person."

Today, the waters of the Ganges River remain sacred to the more than 850 million Hindus worldwide. They believe the waters heal the body, grant wishes, and promise eternal life for the spirit.

The Mogul Empire

The Mogul Empire (1526 to 1857) began when a prince named Babur invaded India from the northwest. Babur's grandson, Akbar, was a great Mogul leader. He ruled from 1556 to 1605. Many of India's most precious works of art date from this time.

Taj Mahal

The Moguls, who were **Muslims**, built grand cities, and many of their monuments and royal tombs can still be seen today. The Mogul emperor Shāh Jāhan honored his wife after her death by building a beautiful large tomb of white marble. It was built between 1631 and 1648 and was later named the Taj Mahal. Twenty thousand laborers worked to construct it. Today, the Taj Mahal is known as one of the most magnificent structures in the world.

The empire lasted for more than 300 years, although it was in decline from about 1700.

Factories, Dams, and European Control

In the late 1600s, many European **industrialists** from England and other countries began building factories along the Ganges River. An industrialist is someone who owns or manages industries. The factories produced great quantities of **textiles** at large profits for their European owners. By the mid-1700s, the British East India Company controlled much of India. The British government

The Mogul emperor Shāh Jāhan built the Taj Mahal in memory of his beloved wife, Mumtaz Mahal.

directly ruled most of India from the mid-1800s until the modern nation of India gained its independence in 1947.

The climate of the Ganges River basin was ideal for growing cotton. During the British colonial period, British engineers built dams to store water in **reservoirs**. Farmers used the stored water to irrigate cotton crops during the dry season. The river basin soon became a center of cotton production and trade.

Crowded Cities

Today, many people live in bustling cities along the banks of the Ganges River and its tributaries. Kolkata, the capital of West Bengal state in India, is the country's second-largest city. It lies on the east bank of the Hugli River, a main branch of the Ganges River in the delta zone. The city was established as a trading port in 1690. Today, it is very densely populated, and many people there live in poverty. However, Kolkata remains an important economic, educational, and cultural center. The city is a major site of manufacturing; industries in or near Kolkata produce automobiles, paper, chemicals, and textiles. The city is also a center for publishing and printing. Kolkata has more than 30 museums and the largest library in India.

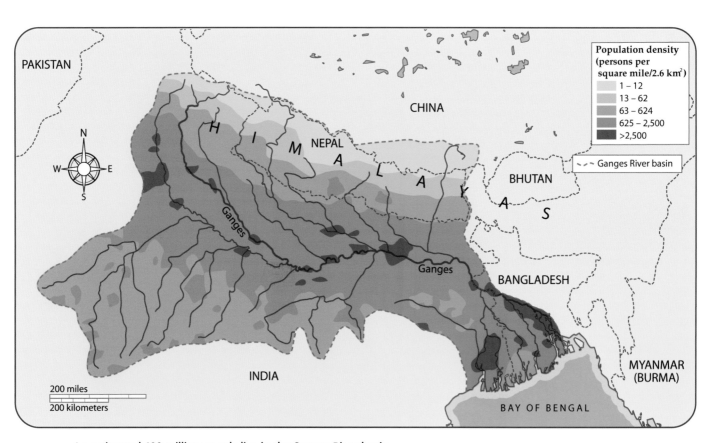

An estimated 400 million people live in the Ganges River basin.

Commuters and shoppers make their way along a crowded street in Kolkata, India.

More than 14 million people live in Kolkata and its suburbs.

In Varanasi, hundreds of temples line the banks of the Ganges River. Each year, more than a million Hindu pilgrims visit the city's bathing ghats, or stone steps that lead down to the river's edge. This holy city, previously known as Benares and Kashi, is an important place of worship as well as a cremation site for Hindus. Varanasi is also a center of art, music, and dance.

CHAPTER 4

Travel and Commerce

The Ganges River has been a major transportation route since ancient times. People used the river to travel between towns and cities. The river also made possible the transport and trade of goods, such as grains, spices, silk, pearls, and cotton.

Boats on the Ganges River

As far back as the sixth century BC, people sailed up the river from the Bay of Bengal to the city of Haridwar. Travel in either direction was easy because of the river's slow current. Ancient boats had sails that could be opened up or rolled down.

The Ganges River was the most important link between the hundreds of towns and cities of northern India. Some goods were stored in port cities and distributed to cities far from the river. Cargo from China and Indonesia arrived at ports on the Ganges delta. Then small boats carried the goods upriver to cities along the Ganges River.

Steaming Through

The introduction of the steamboat in the 1800s transformed trade along the Ganges River. Large steam-powered ships carried tons of cotton and other products down the Ganges River to seaports and then between India and Great Britain. Goods could be transported at speeds much faster than those achieved by boats with sails.

LEFT: Selling spices at a market in India.

This model shows the kind of steamboat commonly used on the Ganges River in the 1800s.

FAST FACT
In the first century BC, India traded with Rome. Indian spices were exchanged for iron tools and other items.

The Ganges Canal

Canals are human-made waterways that are used for shipping and irrigation. They may take in water from natural rivers along their courses. The Ganges Canal was built by British engineers to irrigate the dry land between the Ganges and Yamuna rivers in northeastern India. When the canal was completed in 1854, it was 170 feet (52 m) wide and 10 feet (three m) deep. Over the past century and a half, the canal system has been greatly enlarged.

For the Tourists

The Gangotri Glacier, in the Himalayas, is one of the most popular destinations for tourists in India. The pure waters of this glacier, which feeds the Ganges River, attract hundreds of thousands of hikers and Hindu pilgrims each year. Roads, hotels, restaurants, and even an airport have been built to accommodate tourists. As a result of **commercialization**, however, garbage and human waste are being dumped into the waters.

Scientists also warn that the Gangotri Glacier has shrunk by more than a half mile (850 m) over the past 25 years. This reduction in size may be a result of **global warming**.

The clear, fast-moving waters of the Himalayan zone bring adventurous

The steamboat was also the fastest and most reliable form of transportation for people who traveled on the river.

Hydroelectric Dams

There are some small **hydroelectric** dams on the Ganges River, but they do not contribute substantially to India's electrical supply. Hydroelectric dams would be a "clean" way to generate electricity, but many people worry that building more dams on the river would have harmful effects. The construction of dams and reservoirs would reduce the amount of silt that the river carries and deposits on farmland. Dams would also reduce the flow of the river and limit navigability.

Tourists and a guide trek onto the Gangotri Glacier.

tourists who want to experience white-water rafting. The Ganges River is popular for canoeing and kayaking, too. Tour companies offer yacht, steamboat, and wildlife-watching cruises along parts of the river.

CHAPTER 5
The Modern Ganges

Today, the Ganges River provides for the physical needs of 40 percent of India's people. Modern irrigation pumps supply billions of gallons of water so that farmers can grow food and other crops year-round. The river provides fish to eat and water to drink. The Ganges River also feeds the spiritual life of about 80 percent of India's population. But the actions of humans have seriously threatened the future of the river and the land around it.

Polluting the Ganges River

Pollution is an enormous problem for the Ganges River—it is one of the world's most polluted rivers. Leather tanneries, chemical plants, textile mills, and other factories dump chemical-filled wastewater into the river through open drains and canals. Untreated **sewage** also goes into the river each day, and millions of cremated and partially cremated bodies enter the waters annually. Hindus believe that the ideal end to life is cremation at one of the three tirthas, after which the remains are placed into the Ganges River.

Destroying the Delta Zone

In addition to industrial waste, millions of tons of fertilizers and **pesticides** used on farmland wash into the Ganges River each year. These and other harmful pollutants eventually reach the

A farmer sprays pesticide onto a field outside the Indian city of Siliguri.

LEFT: The historic Ganges River is one of the world's most polluted waterways.

Bengal Tiger

The Bengal tiger, India's official animal, is highly endangered. Poachers hunt and kill the animal for its beautiful orange, black, and white coat. It is also killed for its body parts, such as bones, which some people use as traditional medicines. Conservation organizations are working to try to eliminate poaching and other threats to Bengal tigers.

The majestic Bengal tiger is endangered in its habitat in the Sundarbans.

FAST FACT

The delta zone makes up only 13 percent of the length of the Ganges River. This zone is subjected to 100 percent of the pollution that enters the river along its course.

delta zone. In terms of **habitat** destruction, the delta zone has suffered more environmental damage than the other zones. Crustaceans, such as crabs, shrimp, and lobsters, take in the pollutants. These chemicals then enter the food chain and are passed along to any animals or humans who eat the crustaceans.

Ganges Action Plan

In 1985, scientists and government officials in India defined a series of steps called the Ganges Action Plan (GAP) to help clean up the Ganges River.

"The Ganges swallows up the ashes of every person as it flows along, rejecting [none],…accepting all."

—*Deep River*, by Shusaku Endo (1993, translated 1994)

The plan outlined the need to build sewage treatment plants, public toilets, and other facilities. Today, the government acknowledges that the GAP has failed to achieve the goal of a cleaner river.

Population Problems and Water Disputes

The populations of India and Bangladesh are growing rapidly. In 1900, the Ganges basin was home to about 100 million people. Today, a population of 400 million puts far greater demands on the river to provide water for drinking, industry, agriculture, and the creation of hydroelectricity.

India and Bangladesh have been engaged in water disputes for more than 50 years. Dams in India affect the flow of water to Bangladesh, leaving less water available for people, farms, and industries downstream. Water shortages are a major problem in Bangladesh, especially during the dry season.

Deforestation

During recent decades, deforestation has increased in the foothills of the Himalayas. Some scientists say the clearing of forested land contributes to flooding and causes the erosion, or washing away, of soil along the Ganges River. Flooding occurs because the removal of trees increases the surface **runoff** from rainfall. Without tree roots to anchor soil, the soil washes into rivers and streams. The Ganges River then carries more sediment to downstream areas, where silt builds up on the river bottom, making the river shallower. This buildup makes navigation more difficult. The buildup of silt may also increase the amount of saltwater that can force its way up the river at its delta. Saltier water can harm wildlife habitats and damage agricultural land.

COMPARING THE WORLD'S RIVERS

River	Continent	Source	Outflow	Approximate Length in miles (kilometers)	Area of Drainage Basin in square miles (square kilometers)
Amazon	South America	Andes Mountains, Peru	Atlantic Ocean	4,000 (6,450)	2.7 million (7 million)
Euphrates	Asia	Murat and Kara Su rivers, Turkey	Persian Gulf	1,740 (2,800)	171,430 (444,000)
Ganges	Asia	Himalayas, India	Bay of Bengal	1,560 (2,510)	400,000 (1 million)
Mississippi	North America	Lake Itasca, Minnesota	Gulf of Mexico	2,350 (3,780)	1.2 million (3.1 million)
Nile	Africa	Streams flowing into Lake Victoria, East Africa	Mediterranean Sea	4,145 (6,670)	1.3 million (3.3 million)
Rhine	Europe	Alps, Switzerland	North Sea	865 (1,390)	65,600 (170,000)
St. Lawrence	North America	Lake Ontario, Canada and United States	Gulf of St. Lawrence	744 (1,190)	502,000 (1.3 million)
Tigris	Asia	Lake Hazar, Taurus Mountains, Turkey	Persian Gulf	1,180 (1,900)	43,000 (111,000)
Yangtze	Asia	Damqu River, Tanggula Mountains, China	East China Sea	3,915 (6,300)	690,000 (1.8 million)

TIMELINE

40–50 million years ago	The Himalayas begin to form.
500 BC–300 BC	People of ancient India begin to cultivate rice.
322 BC	The Mauryan Empire begins.
272 BC	King Aśoka encourages the ideals of Buddhism.
450 AD–1200 AD	Agriculture expands throughout India.
1526	The Mogul Empire begins.
1757	With the Mogul Empire in decline, the British East India Company rules much of India by this time.
1800s	Steamboats begin traveling on the Ganges River.
1854	The Ganges Canal is completed.
1858	Direct British rule in India begins.
1900	The population of the Ganges basin reaches 100 million.
1947	India gains independence from Great Britain. Part of British India becomes the separate country of Pakistan.
1950s	Population and industry begin to grow dramatically along the Ganges River.
1971	The independent country of Bangladesh (formerly East Pakistan) is created.
1985	The Indian government initiates the Ganges Action Plan to try to clean up the river.
1996	The prime ministers of India and Bangladesh sign a treaty on the sharing of Ganges River water.
2000	Torrential monsoon rains and raging rivers cause the worst flooding in decades in northern India.

GLOSSARY

archaeologists Scientists who study the material remains (such as fossils and artifacts) of past human life and activities

Buddhist Someone who follows the religion based on the teachings of Gautama Buddha

canals Human-made waterways that are used for shipping and irrigation

commercialization The selling of a product or service as a business for profit

confluence The flowing together of two or more streams

cremation The act of burning a dead body into ashes

cultivation The preparation of soil to grow crops

delta A triangular or fan-shaped area of land at the mouth of a river

dendritic Branching like a tree

drainage basin The area of land drained by a river and its tributaries

drainage pattern The arrangement of a main stream and its tributaries

economic Relating to the way money and goods are produced, consumed, and distributed

ecosystems Complex communities of organisms and their environments functioning as a unit

Eurasian Relating to a single landmass made up of Asia and Europe

glaciers Large bodies of ice and snow moving slowly down a slope or spreading outward on land

global warming A gradual worldwide increase in the average temperature of Earth's atmosphere

gorge: A narrow canyon with steep walls

habitat: The environment in which a plant or an animal naturally lives and grows

headstreams Streams that form the sources of a river

Hindus People who follow Hinduism, the dominant religion of India

hydroelectric Relating to the production of electricity by the movement of water

industrialists People who own or manage manufacturing or other businesses

irrigation The watering of land in an artificial way to foster plant growth

monsoon The season in India and adjacent areas that is characterized by very heavy rainfall

Muslims Followers of the religion of Islam, who believe in Allah as the sole deity and in Muhammad as Allah's prophet

pesticides Chemicals used to kill insects and other pests that harm crops or other plants

pillars Decorative columns standing alone as monuments

poachers People who kill or take wild animals illegally

reservoirs Artificial lakes where water is collected and kept for use

runoff Water from rain or snow that flows over the surface of the ground and into rivers

sediment Material deposited by water, wind, or glaciers

sewage Refuse liquids or waste matter usually carried off by sewers

silt Small particles of sand or rock left as sediment

textiles Woven or knit cloth

tributaries: Smaller rivers and streams that flow into larger bodies of water

FIND OUT MORE

BOOKS

Bowden, Rob. *The Ganges.* Hodder Wayland, 2007.

Sperling, Vatsala. *Ganga. The River That Flows From Heaven to Earth.* Bear Cub Books, 2008.

Spilsbury, Louise, and Richard Spilsbury. *Living on the Ganges River.* Heinemann-Raintree, 2007.

Spilsbury, Richard. *Settlements of the Ganges River.* Heinemann-Raintree, 2005.

Kalman, Bobbie. *India the Land (Revised edition).* Crabtree Publishing Company, 2010.

WEB SITES

Dolphins-World.com: Ganges River Dolphin
www.dolphins-world.com/Ganges_River_Dolphin.html

PBS: The Story of India
www.pbs.org/thestoryofindia/gallery/photos/4.html

The Water Page: River Ganges
www.africanwater.org/ganges.htm

World Wildlife Fund: Ganges River Dolphin
www.worldwildlife.org/species/finder/gangesriverdolphin/gangesriverdolphin.html

ABOUT THE AUTHOR

Molly Aloian has written more than 50 nonfiction books for children on a wide variety of topics, including endangered animals, animal life cycles, continents and their geography, holidays around the world, and chemistry. When she is not busy writing, she enjoys traveling, hiking, and cooking.

INDEX

Page references in **bold** type are to illustrations.